AND IT'S HELLO FROM HIM

Ian Davidson is The Two Ronnies' script editor
and the editor of this book; he also writes and
directs for the stage and television. His theatre
work includes 'A Day in Hollywood, A Night in
the Ukraine' and Barry Humphries' 'Housewife
Superstar'. He has worked on many successful
television comedies with such varied talents as
David Frost, Terry Jones and Mike Palin, Les
Dawson, Kelly Monteith and The Two Ronnies.
His hobby is VAT.

Other Two Ronnies books in Star

THE TWO RONNIES
AND IT'S HELLO FROM HIM

Edited by
IAN DAVIDSON

Illustrations by
IAN HEATH

Star

A STAR BOOK
published by
the Paperback Division of
W. H. ALLEN & CO. LTD

A Star Book
Published in 1980
by the Paperback Division of
W. H. Allen & Co. Ltd
A Howard and Wyndham Company
44 Hill Street, London W1X 8LB
Reprinted 1980
Reprinted 1981

Printed in Great Britain by
Hunt Barnard Printing Ltd., Aylesbury, Bucks.

ISBN 0 352 30796 X

It's those men again . . .

On from strength to strength into another series of programmes go the Two Ronnies O.B.E.

Here's the stuff that makes the office and the pub laugh again on the day after the show—the Ronnies' news.

A bookful of the best of the news from their latest programmes. Plus some that viewers never heard.

Shhh! The countdown's started in the studio, the audience's already smiling . . . ten seconds, nine, eight, seven . . . if you were thinking of nipping outside, it's too late now . . . three, two, one . . . Cue!

GOOD
EVENING

Ronnie Corbett: It's nice to be with you
once again, isn't it Ronnie?

Ronnie Barker: Yes it is. And in a packed programme tonight we'll be meeting the lucky man who bought his drama loving girlfriend 'Selections from Shakespeare'—and got the complete works in return.

RC: And we'll be meeting an impoverished ex-member of the KGB, Smeagol Gollum, who's trying to make ends meet by taking in brain-washing.

RB: In Lonely Hearts Corner, we'll be introducing you to a personable, slim, middle-aged but deeply pessimistic man who wishes to meet a mature attractive woman with a view to possible headaches later.

RC: Though we're very disappointed that we won't meet Ivan Bedlinov after his big win earlier tonight in the World Pickle Eating Championships. He was going to rush here straight after an interview on ITV but apparently he's afraid of repeating himself.

RB: On the other hand, we will be having a word with the shortsighted and rather angry sewage worker who always gets hold of the wrong end of the stick.

RC: And with the London man who leaves unravelled lavatory paper all over the bathroom every morning because he likes to take the tube to work.

RB: And with the amazingly successful award winning Young Businessman of the Year, Kurt Schmetters, who flattens supermarket trolleys and sells them in pairs as air conditioned roller skates.

RC: We will be looking at a new art form which is sweeping America. It involves a mirror and a chair with no seat—so you can draw your own conclusions.

RB: And Roy Gutcrusher Hotchkiss will be here to give a demonstration of solo wrestling—provided he can get a grip on himself.

RC: I'll be having a word with a gay gangster about his fairy godfather.

RB: And with a stickler for tidiness who even puts a sheet of newspaper under the cuckoo clock.

RC: And with the devout Catholic who walked down Blaydon High Street this morning punching women, kicking dogs and swearing because he was going to confession and was short of material.

RB: And with Liza Stoat, the World's Worst Cook, who yesterday scored a new first when she burnt the tin opener.

RC: And I hope we will have time to tell you about the boom in travelling chess sets and show you that even in the back of a Mini you can mate in fifty-six moves.

BUT FIRST,
THE NEWS...

RB: A farmer in Devon has
successfully crossed his main
crop with a masochist and got
corn that thrashes itself.

RC: And an amateur biologist who crossed the seven foolish virgins with the seven deadly sins has got himself forty-nine dirty weekends.

RB: A man crossed a rose with a rabbit and now there's a sucker born every minute.

RC: And a man crossed an Irish spinster with the Potato Marketing Board to get a woman who's grateful for small Murphies.

RB: A misguided scientist crossed a cat and a gorilla—and now it puts him out at night.

RC: And mad scientists who've crossed Danny La Rue with Spotty the Incontinent Dog got a surprise package on Mother Kelly's Doorstep.

ON A MORE SERIOUS NOTE...

RB: Guerilla forces have tonight been forced out of most of the border town of Nya-zum-wadi-ban-bwe-zi but are reported to be hanging on to the last two syllables.

RC: And MI5 admitted today to having a Dirty Tricks department. It's staffed by a one armed soot juggler and three St Bernards who haven't been housetrained.

RB: Meanwhile, news tonight that
        the Army Junior Leaders
        expedition to Borneo has
        suffered a sad depletion of
        numbers. Cannibals have
        already had three hard-boiled
        sergeants, two half-baked
        corporals and a raw recruit.

RC: There's growing concern in
        Leicestershire about a lunatic
        who thinks he's a tent and has
        been knocking at doors asking
        people if they can put him up
        for the night.

RB: The Thames Conservancy's
        claim that the river is fresh as
        far up as Teddington was
        confirmed this afternoon at
        Kingston when a cod was
        caught wrapped in today's
        newspaper.

RC: We've just had a report that an
        Irishman who wanted to go to
        his grandmother's funeral today
        told his boss that his football
        team had died.

RB: News also today that Ernest Grimble, the unlucky home improver who put in storage heaters just before the price of electricity went up, changed to oil just before the Middle East crisis, and finally installed solar panels has now at the end of the first quarter got a bill from God.

RC: Today also saw the opening of the Annual Conference of the Society of Plumbers, Decorators and Handymen at the Royal Albert Hall. It was five days late, delegates claiming that they had called round several times but failed to find anybody in.

RB: Finally, there was an incident at Sheffield's Hartop Road sewage plant today when a main pipe burst and twenty workers were declared repugnant.

RC: But now in the following sketch, entitled the James Boys, James Mason will play a mason, James Fox will play a fox and James Burke appears as himself . . .

THE MAN NOW STANDING IN THE POLICE STATION...

RB: A thief broke into Hetton-le-
        Hole police station today and
        stole all the officers' spectacles.
        Police wish to interview a dark
        grey blur.

RC: Police were today investigating a burglary at the home of retired rag and bone man Arthur Totter, in which a lifetime's collection of paintings and antiques was stolen. A distraught Mr Totter told reporters that the value of the missing property could be in the region of fifty thousand balloons and a goldfish.

RB: Dublin police today raided the studio of Ireland's most brilliant art forger and took away 33 canvasses all signed by Pisscarco.

RC: And West London police wish to alert local residents about the activities of the infamous cross-eyed burglar. If you see this man staring in your windows, warn the people next door.

RB: Here is a police message.
Scotland Yard wish to trace a
gogo girl named Lulu who had
a heyday last Mayday. She put
a voodoo on a Zulu when she
danced the can can on a tom
tom wearing just a tutu with a
pompom going dingdong. She
was last heard of having a bit
of yoho on a lilo and going bye-
byes with some Ities.

RC: An unfortunate fire at New
Scotland Yard today destroyed
hundreds of criminal records,
including *Deck of Cards* by
Max Bygraves.

RB: But now a sketch in which Mr
Ronnie Corbett sings a
sentimental song aimed to
appeal to the Japanese family
man—My Yiddische Yamaha.

HARRY BENNETT, THE
UNDERWORLD'S GREATEST
RECEIVER OF STOLEN GOODS,
WAS KILLED TODAY. HE FELL OFF
THE BACK OF A LORRY.

THE HOME SIDE
ARE EASILY
RECOGNISABLE
IN THE 22% DACRON,
FIGURE HUGGING,
DOVE-GREY AND
CITRON MIX N'MATCH
HEAVILY SPONSORED
STRIP...

RB: Sport. We have just heard that the Irish Indoor Athletic Championships have been called off because it's a nice day ... Whilst at this afternoon's Tipperary Games, in the final cf the tug-of-war, both teams were disqualified for pushing.

RC: The go-slow of jockeys continues. Last Monday's 3.30 at Cheltenham has just finished and the stewards have called for an oil painting to decide the winner.

RB: In Mexico City tonight the last man home in the slow bicycle race of the 1968 Olympic Games was slightly injured when they changed the stadium into a block of flats.

RC: Here's some late football
        news ... the Collier Row
        Wanderers and Hypochondriacs
        United game has just gone into
        the second hour of injury time.

RB: And here's a late football result
        from Siberia. Wolves 4 Sheep 0.

RC: But now a sketch in which I play the part of a porter who works at Victoria Station.

RB: And I play the angry shop steward who catches him at it.

THE COURT WILL RISE...

RB: At the Dublin bankruptcy court this morning, Ireland's worst gambler admitted to losing his last £600 on the St Leger. He lost £200 on the race and £400 on the action replay.

RC: Clapham magistrates fined a young couple today for committing an act of gross indecency in the High Street. They were told to use a bit of common in future.

RB: At his Old Bailey trial today Slasher Nobbs provided a very long alibi signed by 3000 people. The prosecution described it as a 'tissue of lies'.

GROSS INDECENCY
ALLOWED
HERE

RC: The Salford man accused of
        stealing a rocket was today
        acquitted by magistrates even
        though the rocket was hidden
        up his shirt all the time. He
        was later let off by the police.

RB: In the High Court today a
        witch filed a paternity suit
        against a baker for giving her a
        bun in the coven.

RC: Whilst Britain's Most
        Unwashed Man was in court
        today where he pleaded not
        guilty to a charge of stealing
        88 lbs of mushrooms. He
        claimed that the police planted
        them on him.

RB: But now a sketch, featuring Mr
        Ronnie Corbett, who in his
        early days was an artist's
        model but had to give it up as
        he had so little to show for it.

THERE'S NO
PEOPLE
LIKE...

RC: Paul Raymond announced his
         new panto today. It's a
         combination of Peter Pan and
         Cinderella called *Fly Buttons*.

RB: And tonight's big theatrical
         award, Most Promising Actress
         of the Year, went to Deidre
         Wallop, after she'd promised
         the entire jury.

RC: While at the Free Trade Hall Manchester tonight an enthusiastic audience heard a new musical composition by two newly-weds; the work has four movements—a largo, an andante for four hands, a molto allegro con spiritu and a hey presto.

RB: Film news ... Raquel Welch has accepted a part in the sequel to *Godfather Two*, it's called *Godfather Three* and she'll be appearing as the two heavies.

RC: Former Black and White Minstrel Mordecai Throat today accused a rival singer of destroying some of his sheet music. He claimed that the other man burst into his dressing room, stamped on his Tut-Tut-Tutsy, grabbed his Polly Wolly Doodle and kicked his Favourite Things.

RB: Miss Lulu Wobblitt, Britain's leading topless tassel dancer, who had her left tassel stolen, today applied to the Union to work as a single act. Later, in a one-sided agreement, she received permission to give the left a rest, as long as she joins the Performing Rights Society.

30

AND NOW THE HEADLINES AGAIN

RC: In an exclusive interview,
Israeli Prime Minister
Menachem Begin today
revealed how he crossed himself
with Mrs Begin and began the
Begins.

RB: And latest news from Camp
David is that Camp Denzil's
calling round at David's flat
after work.

RC: It was revealed today that five Devonport girls are to go on trial in Baghdad. Sheikh Fuad el Jimjam can have his money back if not fully satisfied.

RB: We've just heard that a Japanese businessman who lost a fortune in the wholesale trade has given it all up and committed Cash'n'Carry.

RC: The Prime Minister was not at home today when a delegation representing the interests of the Boy Scouts, the Fat, Cigarette Smokers and Unmarried Mothers called at 10 Downing Street this afternoon. 'We'll try again tomorrow,' said a spokesman for Up the Scout, Up the Stout, Up the Snout and Up the Spout.

RB: Librarian of the Year Elspeth Pickles has at last had her baby. It was a month overdue and was fined 48p.

RC: And there's a shock conclusion
        in today's report published by
        the Irish Government's Think
        Tank. They've decided they're
        wasting their time . . .
        Following predictions of power
        cuts in this coming winter,
        Irish farmers today rushed to
        market and panic-bought
        battery hens.

RB: Painter Dougal Wicks arrived
        at tonight's Furniture Design
        Centre Fancy Dress Ball
        completely swathed in tinfoil
        with castors on both feet and a
        black velvet cushion on his
        head. He won a consolation
        prize for making a complete
        stool of himself.

RC: In Spofforth today, the funeral
        of Britain's most successful
        door-to-door salesman was
        called off because every time
        they tried to close the lid, he
        jammed his foot in it.

RB: And this year's Most Considerate Husband Award has gone to Mr Jeff Jarvis of Stoke whose wife needs twelve hours' sleep a night, so he lets her hit him with the rolling pin before he goes down the pub.

RC: Finally, bad news now about the Third Division Borneo team who fell into the hands of cannibals. When rescuers arrived, the tribe had eaten all eleven players and were warming up the substitute.

REMEMBER THE POST CODE - THEN EAT IT

RC: Wonderful news. Last year the
       Post Office received nearly five
       billion complaints by letter or
       phone and are now back in the
       black.

RB: Popping through your letter
         box tomorrow morning will be a
         little message from the Post
         Office promising you much
         faster services in 1976.

RC: To commemorate a hundred
         years of the Kennel Club,
         there's a new set of novelty
         stamps depicting Man's Best
         Friends. They lick you.

RB: And latest in a long line of Post
         Office new ideas comes the
         Question phone. This is a spin-
         off of the Answer phone and
         asks you why you're wasting
         your money ringing somebody
         who's out.

GETTING IT TOGETHER

RC: The Yorkshire miner whose wife operates the pithead gear at his colliery is in trouble again for making love when he should have been working. He was pulled up for it fifteen times last week.

RB: Married today were the happy
couple who started their
courting in a launderette soon
after they found their clothes
were going around together.

RC: There was a touching scene this
afternoon at 29 Pudney
Crescent, Knottley, when
Britain's Top Postman, Lance
Duggleby, carried his newly
wed bride up to the front door.
He folded her in four and
shoved her through the
letterbox.

RB: Happy news tonight from Lord
George Davidson's Circus. The
tattooed lady is pregnant and
both she and her husband, the
India Rubber man, are very
happy. They don't mind if it's a
boy or a girl as long as it fits
into the cannon.

RC: Whilst at Caxton Hall today,
the Invisible Man was finally
married to the Invisible Lady.
Afterwards, they posed happily
for radiographers.

RB: And good news too from the proud young woman who nine months ago took a saccharin instead of the Pill and has just had the sweetest baby.

RC: And we've just heard that Swedish Massage Parlours Ltd. have merged with the Womens Royal Voluntary Service to provide feels on wheels.

DECORATIONS WILL BE WORN, LOUNGE SUITS SLIGHTLY WORN...

RC: At a novelty dinner dance in
        Halesowen tonight, everybody
        had a slice of Battenburg before
        the cakewalk, a poultry paté
        was followed by the Turkey
        Trot, while the prune and
        rhubarb pie led to a general
        excuse-me.

RB: The entire staff of Pickfords packed the Albert Hall tonight. Later they all got drunk and gift wrapped Nelson's Column.

RC: And at this afternoon's Braille Society show, a Dundee cake fell off its stand, rolled onto the next stall and won the short story competition.

RB: It was a glamorous night tonight throughout London's West End with the Brassiere Makers Federation holding an enormous gathering, the Brewers Federation having a hop, the Willing Girls Society having a do and Mrs Whitehouse having a don't.

RC: And tonight's Weightwatchers Conference at Earls Court featured Cyril Smith, Tessie O'Shea, Lord Goodman and Orson Welles. The audience had to go to Olympia.

LET NO JUDGEPERSON PUT ASUNDER...

RB: In the divorce court today, Mr Narcissus Beauregard, the Vainest Man in Britain, gained a divorce from his wife on the grounds that whenever he looked in the mirror she threw a bucket of water over them.

The will of City supporter and hooligan Ruari Dimsdale, published today, requests that his ashes be scattered over a United supporter.

RB: The wife of a man who never
        learnt the difference between a
        brassiere and a brazier was
        granted a divorce today on two
        counts. First because when she
        wanted underwear for
        Christmas he gave her two big
        rusty tins with holes in and
        second because of the way he
        kept trying to roast his
        chestnuts.

RC: Yesterday, Mrs Araminta de
        Lesseps, a Herefordshire
        housewife separated from her
        husband, took him to court for
        maintenance. Tomorrow his
        girlfriend is taking him to a
        garage for an MOT.

THE INTERESTING PEOPLE WHO ARE IN TOWN TONIGHT

RD: Later we'll be meeting the lazy housewife who left a note for her husband saying his salad was in the garden.

RC: And we will be having a live link-up with Britain's rudest doctor—direct from his Harley Street Insulting Rooms.

RB: We'll be having a word with Serbo-Croat tourist Josep Mihailovich Djilas Princip who got two tickets for parking in the West End this morning and has been going round the theatres to find out where it's on ever since.

RC: Then Miss Muffet will be here to tell us that today she shared her curds with little Jack Horner and then had her whey with him.

RB: Mr Sydney Garstang, the first man to be appointed an official Town Drunk, will be telling us about his job. He says the money's good but the responsibilities are staggering.

RC: Then we'll meet the karate instructor who gets a miserable salary but plenty of backhanders from his pupils.

RB: We shall be interviewing a happy trade unionist who had dinner at a recent TUC Congress—and we'll be interviewing an even happier trade unionist who had congress at a recent TUC dinner.

RC: Then I'll talk to an impoverished tight-rope walker who's living on a shoestring.

RB: And we'll be hearing about Marcel Gobigny, president of the second French Republic and amateur contortionist, who decorated himself with the Legion d'Honneur, did a back somersault for joy and kissed himself on both cheeks.

RC: And there'll be time for a word with the D I Y enthusiast who's only got one vice—on the bench in the shed in the garden—with the woman from next door.

RB: We were hoping to bring you Flexo the Nude Contortionist but he took a step back at rehearsal this afternoon and stood on his dignity.

RC: Finally, I have a note here
which the BBC typists have
asked me to read out ... "We
are helding oor Animal Dinner
and Dunce at the Savaloy
Gorilla tomorrow ovening.
There will be damping to the
excitig Sod Lawrence
Orchestra, and mudnight
cabaret with the Inedible
Motherhood of Bran ...
R.S.Q.P.

54

FUR AND FEATHER

RC: The Carshalton vet who said today that Britain's cats were fat, lazy and ugly was in hospital tonight after being mogged.

RB: Officials at Haywards Heath Zoo stepped up their search for a mate for poor homesick Brutus, their lonely sex starved male elephant, after he was found earlier today trying to board a Jumbo at Gatwick.

RC: Pathetic news, too, tonight
        from the Mammal House at the
        London Zoo, that Ernest, the
        short-sighted skunk, has fallen
        in love with a gas leak.

RB: There are renewed calls to cull
        the stork with a mean streak
        after he delivered triplets to a
        house where the washing
        machine's broken down.

RC: Colonel Bill Lomax, the world's
        greatest elephant tracker, was
        buried today. In future, he's
        decided not to follow so close
        behind the elephant.

RB: But now a sketch featuring Mr Ronnie Corbett whose lovely wife yesterday heard about a gadget which cuts housework in half so she's written off for two of them.

Yesterday Conrad Trellis celebrated sixty years of non-drinking, non-gambling celibacy. Today he was run over by a brewer's dray that had swerved to avoid a man carrying a fruit machine out of a massage parlour.

THE DELAY IS DUE TO THERE BEING PASSENGERS...

RC: B.R. today announced a new
service for men in dirty old
raincoats entitled the Please-
Put-It-Away-Day.

RB: Latest bulletins say that the porter who sat on a red hot cinder at Kings Cross station is making good progress. He was right on time as he steamed through Newcastle.

RC: There was an ugly moment at Euston Station today when Harold Trodd, British Rail's longest serving porter, received a surprise retirement gift from his colleagues. The Station Master handed Harold a beautiful set of matching luggage and Harold asked him what he thought the bloody trolleys were for.

CAUTION —
MONGRELLOLOGISTS
AT WORK

RB: Later tonight we'll meet a man who crossed a budgerigar with an after six phone call and got a cheap trill.

RC: And a man who crossed an old U-boat with a duck to give a submarine that only comes up for bread.

RB: And then we talk to a young hairdresser in Ealing who's crossed a fairy with a tickling stick to get Nancy with the Laughing Face.

RC: ... crossed a raver with a dumb owl to get a girl who doesn't give a hoot after dark.

RB: ... crossed haddock with a toadstool and came up with a packet of fish fungus.

RC: ... crossed the Atlantic with the Titanic and got halfway.

RB: ... crossed a gay Conservative with a very young Liberal to give a Fairy Tory with a nappy ending.

RC: And crossed a red light and a plastic bag to get a brotheliser.

RB: Finally, a very lazy Gordon Highlander will be telling us how he crossed a bag of flour with his uniform and invented the self-raising kilt.

....AGAIN WITH CAPTIONS FOR THOSE NOT-SO-FAST-ON-THE-UPTAKE

RB: In Bournemouth this afternoon, Mr Dennis Healey mistakenly opened a Conservative Fete. He was, however, given the full red carpet treatment. He was slung over the clothes line and beaten for twenty minutes with a stick.

RC: Gardening expert Humbert
Ratt revealed today that his
brilliant pioneering work with
giant marrows had gained him
five gold medals and a hernia.
However, he has now switched
to pumpkins and has already
developed two new strains.

RB: There was confusion tonight at
the Odeon Cinema, Workington,
when Alma Nibbs, the senior
usherette, accidentally sat on
her torch and showed herself up
in the circle.

RC: Charlie Girosi, best known as
Bimbo the Clown, took his Mini
back to the makers today
because one of the doors
would't fall off.

RB: And there was a nasty scene in a Halifax hairdressers today when a barber accused of clumsiness tried to cut his throat and accidentally shaved himself.

RC: Finally, Scots inventor Dougal Gratton, the man who's designed a car that doesn't need petrol, is now building a road that's downhill all the way from Edinburgh to London.

RB: Traffic news. A juggernaut carrying treacle has overturned on the M4. Drivers are asked to stick to the inside lane.
But now a sketch featuring Mr Ronnie Corbett who used to be a model husband but just the other day took up with a Cindy doll.

TAKE-HOME PAY FALLS BELOW TAKE-PUB PAY

RC: There was an ugly moment today at the Kilburn Biograph Cinema when Job Centre veteran Seamus Killick applied for the job of Projectionist. He was asked to fill in a questionnaire so he went outside and punched the doorman.

RB: Various groups of workers
        voted yesterday on new pay
        deals. Manicurists accepted
        their new package by a show of
        hands, strongmen by a show of
        strength, and toolmakers in a
        secret ballot.

RC: The Queen's Award for
        Industry today went to a
        Rainham firm that has
        successfully sold huge numbers
        of corner cupboards to
        Eskimos.

RB: News tonight that the latest
        threat from the Japanese
        Electronics Industry is a
        surgical truss cum calculator
        which means you can count on
        your own support.

RC: And redundancies are predicted
        over the next five years as
        British Rail is to replace its
        porters with machines that
        don't work.

INSIDE
INFORMATION

RB: Bad news now for those of you in the Isle of Wight. Masher Golding, Britain's Number One Graffitist, was released from Parkhurst this afternoon and is now painting the town.

RC:	Recaptured on a forty-seven bus today was G.B.H. Nutter, the man who broke out of jail on Monday after spending thirty years inside. He gave himself away by standing up for a lady.
RB:	In Dublin tonight, Seamus O'Dowda gave himself up after tunnelling out of jail and told mystified police officers that he was only practising for the big breakout at the end of the month.

TYRE KICKERS' CORNER

RC: A new car accessory went on the market today. It's a blonde who lies on the back seat and nods her head up and down.

RB: A series of mishaps today at Harlesden Driving Test Centre. Learner Driver P. J. O'Rourke dented two cars and punctured the tyres of a third before successfully completing his application form.

RC: A firm in Ilford has hit on a
        novel idea for getting its
        hundred employees to work on
        time. They've reduced the
        spaces in the car park to
        eighty.

RB: Good news for North London
        motorists. Congestion on the
        North Circular Road is to be
        eased by the construction of the
        Golders Green Passover.

RC: Whilst in Carnoustie, a man
        who took the advice of the
        Road Safety Council to wear
        something white at night and
        went out completely in white
        has been run over by a
        snowplough.

RB: Finally, over-zealous traffic
        warden Dymphna
        MacQuorqudale had to jump
        out of the way of a steamroller
        today. She tried booking the
        driver for speeding but was told
        it only went at eight miles an
        hour, she tried booking him for
        not having a seat belt but was
        told that didn't apply. She
        finally nailed him for having
        three bald tyres.

IT'S HELLO, HELLO, HELLO FROM HIM

RB: Samantha Plim, the promiscuous policewoman from Plumstead who had admitted to having her way with all the officers in the Division bar two, was this afternoon carpeted by the Chief Constable, which leaves only one.

RC: The Crown public house in Aberdeen had its charity pile of pennies stolen today. Police said the thieves will not get far, as both coins are marked.

RB: The Irish Mafia have replaced their Godfather. He kept making offers nobody could understand.

RC: Whilst the hunt for the two Irishmen who stole a bunch of pillar box keys last night ended this morning. The police were waiting for them when they made the nine o'clock collection.

RB: Meanwhile, Worthing police are anxious to interview a man who has been selling defective hearing aids door to door. Will anyone who can give any information please ring Worthing 259 and shout for Inspector Harkins.

RC: Further developments tonight in the case of the Hyde Park flasher—the man who jumps out in front of lady joggers stark naked. Eye witnesses have helped police put together an Identikit picture of his face but they are still not sure of his whereabouts.

RB: And we've just heard that the two policemen involved in a high speed chase with a gay burglar on Wimbledon Common, have got away safely.

RC: Scotland Yard's new surveillance methods led to a mix up at Waterloo this morning when some petty thieves realised what was going on. Police stopped bugging the muggers and mugged the buggers instead.

RB: And now a sketch featuring Mr Ronnie Corbett who last week got into the wrong pair of wellington boots and was reported missing.

THEY SMILE WHEN THEY ARE SAD

RB: Punk star Stan Vomit, interviewed today by *19* magazine, said he didn't have a particular girl friend. In fact, she was as far from particular as it's possible to be.

RC: Whilst Miss Raquel Welch, in
        an American television
        interview today, talked about
        the advantages she'd had in her
        acting career. She admitted
        that her bust had opened doors
        for her.

RB: A major insurance company has
        just announced that several
        leading show business
        personalities have insured parts
        of their anatomy. If he damages
        his hands, Liberace will receive
        a million pounds. If he loses his
        teeth, Ken Dodd will get a
        million pounds. Rudolph
        Nureyev will get a lump sum.

RC: News tonight that the popular
        programme *Desert Island Discs*
        is to be revamped. Guests will
        now be asked which eight disc
        jockeys they would choose to
        send to Devil's Island.

RB: Following pressure from the
        Australian Musicians' Union,
        the Sydney Symphony
        Orchestra is to get rid of its
        British players. So tonight is
        the Last Night of the Poms.

RC: At the British Tap Dancing
        Society's Annual Dinner
        tonight, guest of honour Fred
        Astaire was about to give a
        demonstration of his skills
        when he fell into the sweet
        trolley. He recovered
        sufficiently to dance with
        pudding on his top hat,
        pudding on his white tie,
        pudding on his tails.

RB: By the way, we had hoped to introduce you to Miss West Indies in her knitted bikini, but just before the show someone pulled a loose thread and unravelled the Bermuda Triangle.

But now a sketch featuring Mr Ronnie Corbett who today landed the title role in a big new film. It's a follow up to *The Stud* entitled *The Cufflink*.

DOCTOR, DOCTOR...

RB: The Department of Juvenile Health today published the results of its enquiry into why children should eat green vegetables. Chiefly, the document reveals, is that if they don't, they won't get any pudding.

RC: Then we'll be talking about the Fair Sex with a doctor—an Ear Nose and Throat man who admits to being a bit of a legman as well.

But first, the news ...

RB: The recently revealed fears of the Minister of Health that the whole medical profession was against him were confirmed tonight. He fainted in Whitehall and three doctors rushed up and tightened his clothing.

RC: The National Health Service's money-saving scheme for Harley Street starts tomorrow. There will only be one stethoscope for the whole street but all doctors will have a party line.

RB: And in an excitingly packed programme tonight, I'll be interviewing the scientists who have managed to produce the Pill in cream bun form. It's so you can eat your cake and have it.

RC: F. G. Pooter, the man who last week visited a psychiatrist because he thought people were taking advantage of him, today finished decorating the consulting rooms.

RB: Britain's Thinnest and Hairiest Man, Arthur Stringbean, the Human Pipecleaner, was rushed to hospital tonight after eating an entire thirty-pound Christmas pudding. Doctors say he should still pull through.

RC: But now a sketch starring Mr Ronnie Barker who last week plied his lady doctor with champagne but got nothing for his pains.

'SPORTSFLASH' COMES TONIGHT FROM THE NUDE OLYMPICS

RB: There was disappointment at the World Fencing Championships in Helsinki tonight when the Irish Team ran out of creosote.

RC: But good news from the World
        Masochistic Games—The
        British team were beaten into
        first place.

RB: The crowd at the Arbroath
        versus Hamilton Academicals
        game failed to disperse tonight
        until the police threatened to
        take a silver collection.

RC: And at the Acacia Avenue
        ground of twice relegated
        bottom-of-the-league Kingsbury
        Wanderers tonight, the team
        changes were announced to the
        crowd. And then the crowd
        changes were announced to the
        team.

RB: Finally, in tonight's Tongue
Twisters Indoor Cricket League
Finals, Peter Piper's Pickled
Peppers Eleven was easily
dismissed by the Leith Police
who then went on to beat
Susie's Seashore seashell
sellers, chase a bug around a
tree, win the cup and polish it
behind the door.

So now, in the following sketch,
I play an Argentinian footballer
who bends a ball round the
wall.

RC: And I play a doctor who breaks
the news to his wife.

BE
UPSTANDING...

RB: At the inquest on Charlie Shanks, the man who went down the road for a packet of pipecleaners, was snatched up by an escaped Golden Eagle, dropped in Tibet, climbed Everest, got lost up the Amazon and then rowed round the world single-handed before flaking out on his own doorstep, the Coroner recorded a verdict of death by adventure.

RC: And at Kilmarnock today a
        man who had bought two
        packets of Woodbines appeared
        before the Procurator Fiscal
        charged with panic buying.

RB: Harold Thrott, the man who
        last week drove his car through
        the window of a Folkestone
        leathercraft shop, was fined £20
        today and had his licence
        embossed.

RC: At the Old Bailey today, a man
        who entered a Bayswater Road
        public convenience and
        smashed a mirror, was given
        the maximum sentence—seven
        years bad luck.

RB: A man was fined forty pounds today for watching the Changing of the Guards in Whitehall. How he got to be anywhere near their changing rooms is still a mystery.

RC: Also at the Old Bailey today, a 250-year-old woman accused of being a witch was acquitted by an all-toad jury.

RB: But now a sketch starring Mr Ronnie Corbett who managed to make himself so unpopular at the Typing Pool Christmas Party that the girls hung him up and kissed the mistletoe.

LATE
NEWS...

RB: Mr Callaghan announced today
that he intends to set foot on
the moon. Michael Foot says he
must be joking.

RC: A streaker ran through the
snow-covered car park of
Television Centre this morning.
He was awarded a Blue Peter
badge.

RB: A clergyman in Cardiff today announced his intention of driving prostitution underground, which is bad news for the man in the street, but good news for miners.

RC: In Epsom today, Mrs Molly Harbottle very carefully backed her car out of the garage and did £800 worth of damage. Her husband had only backed it in ten minutes before.

RB: Andy MacGowan, the sailorman whose family kept a light burning for him in the window for 30 years, returned home to Perth today—to one of the biggest electricity bills ever seen.

RC: And news tonight that art experts with X-ray equipment have identified the source of the Mona Lisa's enigmatic smile. She's sitting on a whoopee cushion.

RB: The only topless bar in Ireland was closed today. Customers kept complaining that the rain was getting in their beer.

RC: And the mystery of the chimney found in the middle of the Sahara Desert was finally explained last night. The Irish engineer read the plans upside down. It was meant to be a well.

RB: Earlier this evening, at Wexford, the All-Ireland Tree Felling Championships were won by tree fellers from Dublin.

RC: From San Francisco comes news of the tourist who tripped and caught his nose in the tramlines. He had to be pushed all the way to the depot before they could get it out.

RB: The anonymous pools winner who fainted at news of his giant win and fell into a vat of plaster of Paris is today said to be set for life.

RC: Out today is a new word game
        for people who can't spell at all.
        It's called Scalarrable.

        But now it's time to meet the
        woman who took a fertility
        drug and was yesterday
        delivered of a bonny bouncing
        seven pound bag of National
        Growmore.

RB: But first, a sketch featuring the
        amazing talents of Mr Ronnie
        Corbett—a man who always has
        to pick up whatever gets
        dropped on the floor because
        he's the nearest.

CHURCH
TIMES

RB: The new Dean of Westminster
was installed at Lambeth
Palace today between the gas
stove and the fridge.

RC: And this Sunday, as part of a
        busy schedule, the Bishop of
        Bath and Wells will open a
        public bath, bless three wells
        and christen a urinal.

COURT CIRCULAR

There was a huge firework
display at Buckingham Palace
tonight. Princess Anne
stubbed her toe.

HERE'S TO THE NEXT TIME...

RB: Next week we'll be talking to a mathematician from Addingham, a wrestler from Nottingham and a plumber from Flushingham—and doing our best to ignore a loudmouth from Effingham.

RC: And we'll have an excerpt from
the Walthamstow Bigamists
Operatic Society's latest
production *Seven Brides for
Two Brothers.*

RB: Then an expert in Oriental
indoor games is going to tell us
of his passion for Mah Jong—as
long as Pah Jong doesn't catch
him at it.

RC: We definitely will be meeting
the Dubliner who thinks that if
British Oxygen come out on
strike we'll all suffocate.

RB: And the Reverend Ian Paisley
will be here to tell us that
cleanliness is next to godliness,
but only in an Irish dictionary.

RC: We'll be meeting a German hydraulics specialist who fell into an electro-plating tank full of chrome and got his pumper nickelled.

RB: And the undernourished Hollywood hell raiser who's been thrown out of more restaurants than he's had hot dinners.

RC: The Treasurer of the Paris Gays Libbers Swop Shop will be here to tell us what you can get for ten francs—six Alberts, three Johns and a Thomas.

RB: And we'll be talking to the clumsy burglar who fears he's lost his touch and so has been told to take things quietly by his doctor.

RC: We'll be meeting a bionic air
hostess who sleeps with the
automatic pilot.

RB: And Angela Rippon will be here
to tell us about her selfish
streak. She did it at four o'clock
in the morning when most of us
were fast asleep in bed.

RC: And there'll be a new feature
entitled 'The Greatest Shock of
my Life' and we'll be hearing
from the one legged Scotsman
in a kilt about the time he was
standing in the lampshade
department at Heals. And then
an assistant came round
putting in light bulbs . . .

          . . . until then, it's goodnight
from me.

RB: And goodnight from him.

PETITION FROM THE WRITERS

We, the undersigned, wish to remain anonymous.

Frank Adey, David Austin and Tom Johnston, Peter Bain, Stanley Bannister, Alec Baron, John Bartlett, Dennis Berson, John Bilsborough, Ray Binns, Ken Boyle, Geoff Brett, Brian Brinded, George Brodie and Mike Perry, Alex Brown, Colin Brown, Peter Brown, Peter Campbell, Philip Campbell, Jonathan Canter, Garry Chambers, Patrick Chaplin, Syd Clark, John Cotterill, Barry Cross, Dave Dutton, Graham Deykin, Roy Dixon and Ken Wallis, Malcolm Drew, Tony Eccles, Myron Edwards, Wyn Edwards, Paul Eldergill, Harry Evans, A. Farrelly, Eric Flitcroft, Ernest Forbes, Phil Gould, Neville Gurnhill, Tim Hopkins, Howard Imber, S. Kidd, Gary Knight, Geoff Leach, Roland Lester, Ed McHenry, Wally McKinley, Tom Magee Englefield, Gerald Mahlowe, Malcolm Mather, Chris Miller, David Newman and Peter Osborne, Anthony Nicholson, Wendy Norton, Mike Paling and John Ellis, Ray Price, Mike Radford, Terry Ravenscroft, Keith Rawnsley and Peter Long, Mike Redfern, Tony Rich, Laurie Rowley, John Sayle, Terry Treloar, Peter Vincent, Len Walker, David Webb, Alan Wightman, Peter Wise, Bob Hedley (co-editor), Cathie Dixon (typist).

P.S. If keeping us anonymous fails, then could we have our names in bigger letters at the end of the programme? And slower so the family can get their reading glasses on?